Original title:
Sunrise Connections

Author: Aron Pilviste
ISBN HARDBACK: 978-1-80560-286-6
ISBN PAPERBACK: 978-1-80560-751-9

Illuminating Connections

In shadows deep where silence dwells,
A spark ignites, a story tells.
Hearts intertwine, with whispers shared,
In this vast world, we've truly dared.

Each glance a bridge, each laugh a thread,
We weave our lives, where kindness spreads.
Together we'll rise, like stars in flight,
Guided by love, through the night.

Day's First Touch

As dawn breaks clear, with gentle grace,
A golden hue begins to chase.
The night retreats, its shadows fade,
In morning's light, new dreams are made.

Birds sing sweet, a song of cheer,
While flowers bloom, their colors near.
With every ray, the world awakes,
Embracing warmth, as daylight breaks.

A New Dawn's Melody

A melody plays in the crisp, cool air,
With every note, we shed our care.
The sun ascends, a bright refrain,
In harmony, we find our gain.

Together we step, to the rhythm of life,
Through joy and sorrow, through peace and strife.
In moments shared, our souls align,
Creating music, pure and divine.

Intertwined in Light

Beneath the stars, we take our flight,
Together we shine, the world ignites.
Hand in hand, through shadows we roam,
In every heartbeat, we find our home.

The tapestry woven, with threads of gold,
Our stories bind, together, bold.
In this embrace, we rise above,
Intertwined in light, we find our love.

Awakening Heartbeats

In the quiet morn's embrace,
Whispers stir and hearts race.
Sunshine peeks through softly,
Life begins anew, so loftily.

Dreams shatter in silver light,
Tremors of hope, taking flight.
Feelings pulse beneath the skin,
Awakening where love can begin.

The Colors of Tomorrow

Brushstrokes of a vibrant hue,
Painting skies in shades so true.
Each moment, a canvas wide,
Futures bloom where dreams reside.

Emerald greens and sapphire blues,
Life's palette rich, we can choose.
With every step, a chance to see,
The beauty in our tapestry.

A Chorus at Dawn

The birds begin their sweet refrain,
Melodies wash away the pain.
In the hush of early light,
Voices rise with pure delight.

Each note a promise whispered clear,
Hope resounds as day draws near.
Together, hearts in harmony,
A chorus shared, wild and free.

Gentle Beginnings

Softly tiptoeing through the day,
Embracing all in a tender way.
Moments linger, sweet and slow,
As the seeds of kindness grow.

Beneath the weight of heavy skies,
New life stirs and softly sighs.
In small gestures, love takes root,
Gentle beginnings bear sweet fruit.

Light's Embrace

In morning's glow, the shadows fade,
A tender touch from sun's soft blade.
Whispers of warmth, they start to rise,
Carrying dreams beneath the skies.

Golden rays dance on the leaves,
Nature hums as the heart believes.
Every petal, every tree,
Embraced by light, they sing with glee.

A world alive, a canvas bright,
The palette shifts with pure delight.
Colors bloom, and spirits soar,
In light's embrace, we seek for more.

The song of dawn, a sweet refrain,
Caressing souls like gentle rain.
As shadows wane, new hopes take flight,
In every heart, there shines a light.

With every breath, we feel the grace,
A warming touch, a sweet embrace.
In light's embrace, we find our way,
Through every night, another day.

Day's Gentle Caress

Softly flows the morning dew,
Kissing petals, fresh and new.
With each ray, a story spun,
Day awakens, a race begun.

Fingers of light dance on the ground,
Embracing life, all around.
A gentle breeze, a sigh, a twist,
Day's caress, too sweet to miss.

Sunlit paths where laughter rings,
A symphony that nature sings.
With every step, our spirits rise,
Touched by warmth beneath the skies.

Golden hours, moments shared,
In daylight's glow, all souls are bared.
Together we find peace and hope,
In daylight's arms, we learn to cope.

As shadows lengthen, day must part,
But echoes linger in the heart.
We gather strength from moments passed,
In day's gentle caress, love is cast.

The Awakening of Hearts

In the stillness of the dawn,
Whispers call, the night is gone.
Hearts arise with the sun's first light,
A promise blooms, hopes take flight.

Through the silence, truths emerge,
Like rivers flow, emotions surge.
Each heartbeat sings a different song,
In the quiet, where we belong.

Beneath the sky, in open fields,
A tapestry of love reveals.
Awakening dreams, vibrant and bold,
In every heart, a warmth unfolds.

Softly spoken, words ignite,
Boundless feelings take their flight.
Together, we weave a sacred trust,
In the awakening, hope is a must.

As day breaks forth, we rise anew,
A world awakened, fresh and true.
With hearts aligned, we forge our way,
In life's embrace, come what may.

Glimmers of Togetherness

In the soft glow of twilight,
We find warmth in shared whispers.
Each star dances above us,
A witness to our quiet joy.

Hand in hand, we traverse the path,
With laughter echoing in the breeze.
The world fades in gentle hues,
As time weaves dreams around us.

In moments rich and quiet,
Love's essence lingers like fragrance.
A tapestry of memories,
Stitched with threads of our laughter.

Through the haze of fading light,
Together, we forge a memory.
In the depths of each glance shared,
Crystal glimmers of forever.

As night embraces our shelter,
We find peace in this stillness.
Heartbeats align in the dark,
And our dreams rise like starlight.

Bonds in the Morning Mist

As dawn breaks with soft whispers,
The mist wraps the world in silence.
Together we greet the day,
With hearts intertwined in hope.

Footsteps on a dewy path,
Each moment a sweet promise.
Sunlight inches through the fog,
Bringing warmth to our quiet bond.

Birdsong flutters like petals,
Dancing in the fresh morning air.
Our laughter mingles with the breeze,
Creating symphonies of joy.

With every sip of warm coffee,
Our thoughts blend in soft colors.
In the glow of this new day,
Trust blooms like flowers in spring.

By the river, we find solace,
Watching reflections of our dreams.
In the cradle of morning light,
Together, we are unbreakable.

Serenity in the Stray Light

In the soft touch of evening,
We wander through shadows and light.
With each step, hearts in sync,
Finding peace in shared silence.

Leaves whisper secrets of ages,
Casting shadows on our pathway.
In stray beams, our laughter lingers,
Carried by the cool night air.

A couch of stars unravels,
Above, the universe watches.
Together, we dream awake,
Painting the night with our stories.

Time, a gentle companion,
Keeps moments wrapped in stillness.
Beside you, I find my place,
In serenity, we are whole.

In this cosmic embrace,
We weave hours like threads of gold.
Bound by whispers of the night,
Together, we are forever.

Conversations in the Radiance

In golden light, our words float,
Like petals carried by the wind.
Thoughts intertwine in whispers,
As the sun dips below the hills.

Each shared story, a treasure,
Unfolding softly like dawn.
With laughter echoing like bells,
Moments bloom in vibrant colors.

The air, thick with sweet promises,
Carries dreams from heart to heart.
In the radiance of our bond,
We build castles in the sky.

As day wanes, shadows deepen,
Yet our light remains unwavering.
Conversations dance in the dusk,
Kindling sparks that never fade.

In the glow of mutual trust,
We find courage in our words.
Together, facing the unknown,
With love, we are never alone.

From Shadows to Splendor

In the quiet folds of night,
Whispers of dreams take flight.
From the dark, a flicker glows,
Shadows dance, while hope grows.

Journey through the untold past,
Where memories are meant to last.
Step by step, the light will rise,
Painting truth across the skies.

Through the mist, the path reveals,
Wounds that time gently heals.
Each heartbeat sings a song,
In this world where we belong.

Colors burst, like spring anew,
Each moment, a vibrant hue.
From despair to sweet delight,
We embrace the morning light.

Together, we rise and soar,
From shadows, we find more.
In splendor's warm embrace,
Our spirits dance in grace.

Mornings Shared

The sun peeks through the trees,
A gentle kiss, a warm breeze.
Coffee brews like dreams unfold,
In morning light, together we hold.

Laughter spills, a joyous sound,
In these moments, love is found.
With every sip, our hearts align,
In this union, you are mine.

The world awakens, colors blend,
Each new day, our hearts transcend.
Hand in hand, we greet the dawn,
In this promise, we carry on.

Birds take flight in the golden sky,
As we watch the morning high.
Together we create our fate,
In these mornings, we celebrate.

Time stands still, the clock will wait,
In your eyes, I see our fate.
Every sunrise brings a chance,
To live, to love, and to dance.

Radiant Journeys

Steps taken on the winding road,
Carrying dreams, a heavy load.
With each mile, the heart expands,
As we journey through these lands.

Mountains high, and valleys low,
In every turn, we learn and grow.
The sky above tints shades of blue,
Every path leads me to you.

Stars above guide our way,
In the night, we choose to stay.
Peaceful moments shared as one,
A radiant journey has begun.

Through the storms, through the calm,
Your laughter is my healing balm.
Together, we face the unknown,
In this light, we have grown.

Hand in hand, we chase the dawn,
With every sunrise, we are drawn.
Embracing all that life can give,
In this journey, we truly live.

When Night Meets Day

As twilight dances with the dawn,
The world awakens, shadows drawn.
Colors blend in a tender sigh,
When night meets day, time slips by.

Stars whisper secrets to the sea,
While the sun wakes, wild and free.
Softly, the horizon ignites,
The blending of our days and nights.

In the stillness, dreams collide,
With every pulse, the worlds abide.
A symphony of light and dark,
In this union, we leave our mark.

Hope emerges, a soft embrace,
In the twilight's gentle grace.
Together in this fleeting play,
We bloom anew in light's ballet.

Through the cycles, life will sway,
In this dance of night and day.
For every ending, there's a start,
A rhythm sung by every heart.

Illuminated Paths

Beneath the stars, we walk the night,
Every step, a whispered light.
The moon above, a guiding friend,
In shadows deep, our fears we mend.

Through tangled woods and winding trails,
A breeze brings forth forgotten tales.
With every turn, adventure calls,
The heart ignites, the spirit sprawls.

This road of dreams, we dare to chase,
In every heartbeat, a sacred space.
Together bound, hand in hand,
On illuminated paths, we stand.

The dawn will break, but first, we roam,
In twilight hues, we find our home.
Through valleys vast and mountains high,
In glowing dusk, our souls shall fly.

Softly Breaking Silence

In tranquil nights, the whispers flow,
The world around us starts to glow.
With every sigh, the heart awakes,
In gentle hush, the spirit shakes.

The stars above, like candles bright,
They pierce the dark, ignite the light.
Each moment wrapped in velvet calm,
A soothing balm, a sacred psalm.

The echoes fade, the stillness stays,
In quietude, the mind obeys.
With every thought, a feathered touch,
In silence deep, we rise so much.

Soft shadows dance, the world conspires,
To weave a tapestry of dreams and fires.
With hearts aligned, we find the grace,
In softly breaking silence, we embrace.

Ties of Morning Glow

The sun climbs high, a golden thread,
In morning's warmth, all doubt is shed.
The roses bloom, their petals spread,
With fragrant whispers, day is fed.

The morning dew like jewels cling,
To every leaf, to every spring.
Nature sings in vibrant hues,
As daylight breaks, we share our views.

In gentle waves, the breezes play,
As laughter rolls, we greet the day.
With hopeful eyes, we seek the sun,
In ties of morning glow, we run.

With arms outstretched, we greet the light,
Casting shadows of the night.
Together bound, our spirits rise,
In morning's glow, we claim the skies.

Fragments of Daylight

In fleeting moments, shadows blend,
The day's embrace, it will not end.
With every glance, a story told,
In fragments of daylight, hearts unfold.

The sun retreats, but hope remains,
In golden streaks, and amber veins.
Each memory glows, a treasure bright,
In fading hues, we find our light.

Through winding paths, we dance along,
In simple joys, we find our song.
With laughter shared, we paint the sky,
In fragments of daylight, we fly.

As twilight descends, we hold it dear,
Each cherished laugh, each whispered cheer.
Together we weave, the day's embrace,
In fragments of daylight, we find our place.

Harmonies at the Break of Day

Rays of light begin to play,
Whispers soft as night gives way.
Birds awaken, songs take flight,
In the dawn, there shines pure light.

Colors blend in morning's breath,
Life stirs gently, wakes from death.
Dewdrops glisten on the grass,
Time, it seems, begins to pass.

Mountains rise, their peaks aglow,
As the sun mounts high and slow.
Nature's chorus sings anew,
In the dawn, our hopes break through.

Moments linger, soft and warm,
In this haven, free from harm.
The world awakens, spirit true,
In the dawn, all feels renewed.

Grateful hearts, we rise and sway,
To the rhythm of the day.
Hand in hand, we find our way,
In this light, forever stay.

Swirls of Golden Promise

Golden hues in skies so bright,
Dance and twirl, a pure delight.
Clouds like brushes, paint the scene,
In this moment, life feels keen.

Fields of wheat in gentle sway,
Chasing shadows of the day.
Promises whispered on the breeze,
Rustling softly through the trees.

Sunset's glow ignites the land,
Nature's canvas, vast and grand.
In the twilight, dreams take flight,
Guided by the coming night.

Stars emerge as dark prevails,
Underneath, the heart exhales.
Hope ignites in silver streams,
Carried forth by whispered dreams.

With every dusk, a dawn will rise,
Swirling light in endless skies.
In the promise of the day,
Life rejoices, come what may.

Embracing the Glimmer

Softly glints the morning dew,
Nature wakes, begins anew.
In the stillness, whispers grow,
Carried forth by winds that blow.

Sunlight kisses hills and trees,
Gentle rustle in the breeze.
Every shadow, every light,
Holds the truth of day and night.

Fingers dance through fields of gold,
Stories of the day unfold.
In the hearts of those who see,
Glimmers of what is to be.

Every heartbeat, every sigh,
Threads the fabric of the sky.
In the silence, secrets hum,
To the song of life, we come.

Embrace the light within your soul,
Let it stretch and make you whole.
In the shimmer, find your way,
Embracing each and every day.

Ushering in the Day

With the dawn, the world awakes,
Birds take flight, a new path makes.
Nature's breath, a gentle sigh,
Underneath the endless sky.

Sunrise paints the hills in hue,
Shadows stretch, then bid adieu.
In the light, we stand anew,
With the chance to seek what's true.

Every heartbeat leads us on,
To the promise of the dawn.
In the stillness, find our grace,
Usher in this sacred space.

Life's a dance, a rhythmic play,
As we greet the light of day.
Hand in hand, we move along,
In this journey, we belong.

Hope ignites with every rise,
Stars retreating from the skies.
In the morning, hearts align,
Ushering in the day, divine.

The Rise of New Bonds

In a world where shadows linger,
Hearts collide and spark anew.
Together they weave a tether,
Stronger than the morning dew.

Whispers of a shared connection,
Promises that boldly shine.
With every thread's reflection,
Hope entwined, your hand in mine.

Over mountains, vast and wide,
The bonds we build will never break.
Through the storms, we stand beside,
In the warmth of love's awake.

Embracing change, we seek to find,
Paths that lead to brighter days.
In this journey, hearts aligned,
Together, we'll find our ways.

As we rise to face the dawn,
Let our spirits soar and twine.
In the light, all fears are gone,
A testament of love divine.

Fading Night's Grace

As twilight whispers soft goodbyes,
A silver glow begins to fade.
The stars retreat from darkened skies,
While dreams of night, in hearts, cascade.

With every breath, the dawn draws near,
Colors blend in vibrant hue.
The echoes of the night disappear,
In the warmth of morning's dew.

With open arms, the day unfolds,
Embracing all that lies ahead.
The stories of the night retold,
In the golden rays we tread.

A silent promise in the light,
To hold the memories made clear.
Fading night gives way to bright,
As hope and joy begin to steer.

So let us dance in morning's grace,
To honor what the night has shown.
For with each dawn, a new embrace,
A tapestry of life we've grown.

Together at Dawn

In the hush of morning's light,
Two hearts wake as one, anew.
With the dawn comes pure delight,
Painting skies in subtle blue.

Whispers carried on the breeze,
Softly spoken dreams take flight.
In each gaze, the world agrees,
Together, we ignite the night.

With every step on dewy grass,
The promise of the day unfolds.
In this moment, time will pass,
Yet our story still is told.

Through the trials that may come,
We will stand, hand in hand, aligned.
In the rhythm, love's sweet drum,
With every beat, our souls combined.

As the sun begins to rise,
Let us chase the shadows away.
For together, under bright skies,
We'll embrace a brand new day.

A Tapestry of First Light

Threads of dawn in colors bright,
Weave a tale of dreams to come.
In the silence, a pure delight,
Nature hums a gentle drum.

Each ray paints the world aglow,
Banishes the night's embrace.
In this moment, feel it flow,
The heartbeat of a sacred space.

From the valleys to the peaks,
Morning washes away the gray.
In this dance, the heart now speaks,
A chorus for a brand new day.

Voices blend, both soft and clear,
Harmonies within our reach.
Every promise held so dear,
Life's own rhythm starts to teach.

With each dawn that we behold,
A masterpiece of hope, we find.
In the tapestry of gold,
We become forever intertwined.

Radiant Beginnings

In the dawn's early light,
Hopes rise like the sun.
Hearts awaken to dreams,
A fresh journey begun.

Whispers of the morning,
Flutter with each breeze.
Nature sings a sweet song,
As all worries ease.

Colors burst in the sky,
Painting worlds anew.
Every moment ignites,
Futures shining through.

Embracing new chances,
With courage we tread.
Each step a new story,
Our spirits widespread.

Together we traverse,
The path laid ahead.
Radiant beginnings bloom,
Where dreams are widespread.

The Dance of Shadows

In twilight's gentle grasp,
Shadows start to sway.
Secrets weave and whisper,
In the fading day.

Silent steps in the dark,
Crafting tales untold.
The moon begins to rise,
Its silver threads unfold.

Each shadow holds a dream,
A story left to share.
Through the night, we wander,
With hearts laid bare.

When the stars start to hum,
We gather in their glow.
Together we embrace,
The magic of the flow.

The dance of fleeting hours,
A timeless serenade.
In the arms of the night,
All our fears do fade.

A New Day Beckons

Awake to the horizon,
A promise softly calls.
Each moment leans forward,
As the starlight falls.

With every breath we take,
We cast aside the past.
The canvas is awaiting,
For colors bold and vast.

The sun breaks with a smile,
Illuminating skies.
Hope dances in our hearts,
As the shadows rise.

Possibilities abound,
In the warm embrace.
A new day calls us forth,
To claim our rightful place.

Together hand in hand,
We walk this path anew.
A new day beckons brightly,
With each venture true.

Where Light Meets Love

In the dawn of affection,
Two souls gently align.
The warmth of their presence,
A spark, tender and kind.

Beneath the vast expanse,
They share a silent glance.
Where light meets love's embrace,
A soul's blissful dance.

With whispers like a breeze,
Their laughter fills the air.
In the quiet moments,
Love's essence lingers there.

As time flows like a river,
Their hearts find home at last.
Where light meets love's promise,
Shadows of the past.

Together they will flourish,
In the warmth that they've found.
Where light meets love eternal,
Their hearts forever bound.

Morning's Palette

Colors burst across the sky,
With whispers of a new reply.
Soft pinks and golds intertwine,
Bringing hope in every line.

Birds awaken with sweet song,
As nature dances all day long.
The world stirs from its dream,
A radiant morning theme.

Dewdrops glisten on the grass,
Each shining jewel a moment to pass.
Leaves sway gently in the breeze,
A tranquil beauty that aims to please.

As the sun climbs higher still,
Warmth envelops, a gentle thrill.
Morning's canvas paints the day,
In vibrant hues that softly play.

Each moment holds a spark of grace,
In this peaceful, waking space.
Time unfurls, a tender sigh,
In morning's arms, we learn to fly.

Ties Woven in Light

Threads of gold weave through the air,
Binding hearts with gentle care.
Moments shared in sunlight's glow,
In every smile, connections grow.

Laughter dances, joy ignites,
In the warmth of shared delights.
Fingers touch, a soft embrace,
In this tender, sacred space.

Bonds that flourish, never fray,
In shadows cast by end of day.
With every heartbeat, love expands,
In the weave of joined hands.

Time may bend, but hearts remain,
In the fabric of joy and pain.
Together, woven, we stand tight,
Ties bound eternally in light.

With every dawn, the threads renew,
Our stories told in every hue.
In the tapestry, joy and strife,
We find our meaning, we find our life.

Gentle Illuminations

Twilight whispers soft and low,
Casting shadows, a gentle glow.
Stars appear, a velvet sigh,
Lighting up the vast night sky.

Moonbeams dance on tranquil waves,
Guiding dreams through night's enclaves.
Each light a story, softly spun,
In the silence, heartbeats run.

Winds carry secrets from afar,
Illuminated by a distant star.
Thoughts unfurl like petals wide,
In this quiet, cosmic tide.

Whispers weave through midnight air,
In this realm, we find our care.
Holding hands, we drift and sway,
In gentle illuminations' play.

Every moment, softly penned,
In the light where shadows blend.
We chase the dreams that glow so bright,
Finding comfort in the night.

Dance of the Dawn

The sun peeks up, a shy debut,
Awakening the world anew.
Colors stretch, as shadows flee,
In the morning's jubilee.

Wind whispers secrets through the trees,
Carrying the scent of blooming peas.
Every petal, dew-kissed bright,
Joins the dance in morning light.

Birds pirouette on branches high,
Celebrating the open sky.
In their song, the day begins,
A melody of gentle sins.

Clouds waltz slowly, soft and free,
Playing hide and seek with the sea.
The world twirls on nature's stage,
In the dance that knows no age.

With each heartbeat, life unfolds,
Stories whispered, mysteries told.
We join the rhythm, hearts awestruck,
In the dawn's embrace, we find our luck.

Morning's Touch

Soft whispers greet the dawn,
A tender light, a gentle yawn.
Birds sing sweetly up above,
Embracing all with morning love.

Dewdrops glisten on the grass,
As shadows fade and moments pass.
Nature wakes with vibrant hues,
A world refreshed, a brand new muse.

The sun ascends, a golden flame,
Reminding us of hope, of aim.
Each ray a promise, bold and bright,
Igniting dreams, dispelling night.

In this hour, hearts start to soar,
With every breath, we long for more.
Morning's touch a soft caress,
A chance to rise, to dream, to bless.

Let us embrace this fleeting time,
Where every moment feels like rhyme.
In the light, our spirits dance,
Awakening to life's sweet chance.

Intertwined Horizons

In the distance, skies collide,
Where colors blend and dreams abide.
Mountains speak with ancient tones,
Whispering secrets in their stones.

At twilight's edge, the stars ignite,
Together they weave day to night.
A canvas vast, both bold and shy,
As earth and sky entwined, they lie.

In every sunset, stories dwell,
Of journeys taken, tales to tell.
Horizons merge, a dance divine,
A bridge uniting yours and mine.

Clouds embrace the waning sun,
In hues of passion, day is done.
We stand in awe, hands intertwined,
Reflecting dreams in hearts aligned.

Beyond the fade, a promise stirs,
In every heartbeat, hope recurs.
Together we shall find our way,
As horizons paint a brand new day.

Daybreak's Promise

The dawn arrives with whispers sweet,
A tender heart beneath our feet.
Sunlight spills in golden streams,
Awakening the world from dreams.

With every ray, new life ignites,
A symphony of pure delights.
Birds take flight in morning's song,
In rhythm where our hearts belong.

The air is fresh, the world anew,
Daybreak whispers, dreams come true.
Underneath the endless skies,
Hope takes root, and fear just flies.

With open arms, we greet the day,
In sunlit paths, we find our way.
Promises linger in the breeze,
Calling forth our hearts with ease.

Daybreak's promise, bright and clear,
A gentle call that draws us near.
Together, we will rise and shine,
In this moment, you are mine.

Colors of Reunion

Brush strokes bright on canvas wide,
Colors mingle, side by side.
Shadows melt, and sorrows fade,
In vibrant hues, our hearts are laid.

Each splash a memory to relate,
In every shade, love resonates.
Silver linings, golden dreams,
In this reunion, nothing seems.

The palette shifts, a gentle sway,
As laughter echoes through the fray.
Connections spark in every glance,
Uniting souls in a joyful dance.

With arms open, we dare to share,
A tapestry woven with utmost care.
Every color, every line,
A masterpiece, where hearts align.

In this moment, we are whole,
In the gallery of the soul.
Together, through the light we roam,
In colors bright, we find our home.

The Light Between Us

In whispers soft, the shadows play,
A glow that guides us on our way.
Through tangled paths, two hearts aligned,
The light between us, gently defined.

With every step, the spark ignites,
Illuminating endless nights.
In silence shared, our souls embrace,
In the radiance, we find our place.

As stars emerge in twilight's hue,
The bond we share feels ever new.
In moments brief, forever spun,
Two souls entwined, a journey begun.

The warmth we hold in tender grasp,
An unseen thread that time won't clasp.
Through storms we rise, unyielding yet,
The light between us, a promise met.

So let it shine, this gift we share,
In every glance, in every prayer.
Though paths may wind and time may bend,
The light between us will never end.

Conversations of Dawn

In quiet morn, the world awakes,
As golden hues the stillness breaks.
With every ray, a whisper flows,
Conversations where the sunlight glows.

The breezes hum a gentle tune,
While nature stirs, beneath the moon.
Each rustle speaks of dreams anew,
In dawn's embrace, the heart breaks through.

The flowers bow, their petals greet,
As melodies in light compete.
In harmony, the day begins,
A dance of joy where hope now spins.

In moments shared, in silent sighs,
The world enchants, as time defies.
And in the glow of morning's breath,
Conversations linger, defying death.

So let us cherish each new day,
In dawn's soft light, we find our way.
With every smile, with every sound,
We weave the threads of love profound.

Threads of Warmth

In woven ties, our spirits meet,
With every stitch, a rhythm sweet.
The fabric holds our stories tight,
Threads of warmth, woven in light.

As seasons change, the colors blend,
In this embrace, the path won't end.
Through storms we've faced, through tears we've shed,
Together, where the heart is led.

With every touch, a memory sewn,
In every laugh, a seed is grown.
The tapestry, a life we share,
Threads of warmth, beyond compare.

In quiet nights, in bold daylight,
Each thread reflects the love's pure light.
Together we create and play,
Threads of warmth that guide our way.

So let us weave, hand in hand,
A work of art, a promise planned.
In every moment, joy reborns,
Threads of warmth, where love adorns.

Radiance in the Stillness

In quietude, the world reveals,
A radiance that softly heals.
In stillness deep, our spirits soar,
A peace that settles at the core.

With every breath, the heart expands,
As time unveils its gentle hands.
In moments lost, we find our way,
Radiance born from night to day.

Each silent echo speaks so loud,
In whispers soft, beneath the shroud.
The stillness wraps around our fears,
Radiance flows, dissolving tears.

So let us pause and find the grace,
In every heartbeat, every space.
For in the quiet, truth will spark,
Radiance shining through the dark.

In every thought, in every sigh,
The stillness lifts our spirits high.
With open hearts, we can embrace,
Radiance in the stillness, our sacred place.

Bonds in the Radiance

In the glow of the morn, we gleam bright,
Hearts entwined, spirits taking flight,
Each moment shared, a treasure we find,
Together in joy, our souls aligned.

Through the trials, we stand tall,
A symphony played, we heed the call,
With laughter and love, we weave our tale,
In the dance of the stars, we shall not fail.

As shadows fall, we hold each tight,
In the warmth of our bonds, we ignite the night,
With every heartbeat, we shine anew,
In the tapestry of life, it's me and you.

In the embrace of the endless sky,
We grow stronger, together we fly,
With dreams that shimmer, and hopes that glow,
In the bonds of radiance, our love will flow.

Rise and Shine Together

Awaken with the sun, a brand-new day,
Side by side, we find our way,
Through fields of gold, and skies so blue,
Hand in hand, just me and you.

With laughter ringing, our spirits soar,
Together we open every door,
In the rhythm of life, we dance and play,
In perfect harmony, we'll find our way.

The world spins fast, but we stand still,
In the power of love, we find our will,
With every dawn, our dreams align,
In the promise of morning, our hopes entwine.

Through all the seasons, we'll stand so strong,
In each other's arms, where we belong,
Together we'll rise, and together we'll shine,
In the light of our love, forever divine.

The Flare of New Bonds

In the twilight, a spark ignites,
New connections bloom like starry sights,
Hearts awakening, a fresh embrace,
In the warmth of the night, we find our place.

With laughter echoing beneath the moon,
Two souls united, a tender tune,
Every glance tells a story untold,
In the flare of new bonds, our dreams unfold.

Together we wander through shadows and light,
Finding each other in the heart of the night,
With every step, we grow and explore,
In this journey of love, we crave for more.

As the stars shimmer, we shimmer too,
In the magic of moments, just me and you,
With hands intertwined, we face the unknown,
In the flare of new bonds, we feel at home.

Coupled with the Light

In the morning glow, we rise as one,
Every shadow fades, the darkness shunned,
With hearts aglow, we embrace the day,
Side by side, we'll find our way.

Through whispers of dreams, we chase the sun,
In laughter and light, our journey's begun,
With each step forward, we pave our track,
In the warmth of our bond, there's no looking back.

Hand in hand, we dance through time,
In the rhythm of love, our hearts chime,
With every sunrise, our spirits align,
Coupled with the light, our love will shine.

The world may change, but we stand fast,
In the embrace of each moment, love's spell cast,
Together we dream, with hearts so bright,
In the glow of our bond, we're coupled with light.

Sunlit Reflections

Golden rays dance on the lake,
Whispers of warmth, they gently wake.
Trees shimmer in the soft embrace,
Nature's mirror, a calming space.

Clouds drift lazily in the sky,
Painting tales as they drift by.
The world glows in a golden hue,
Reflecting dreams, both old and new.

In this moment, worries cease,
The heart finds solace, peace, and ease.
Each ripple tells a story sweet,
In sunlight's glow, all souls meet.

Children laugh on the grassy shore,
Their joy, a symphony to adore.
Life unfolds in a gentle sway,
Under the sun, in bright array.

As dusk approaches, hues turn bold,
A tapestry of stories told.
In twilight's grace, let us unite,
In sunlit reflections, pure delight.

Early Echoes of Unity

Morning whispers in fresh air,
Unity arises with gentle care.
Birds sing sweetly, a chorus bright,
Binding hearts in the soft dawn light.

Footsteps weave through meadows green,
A shared journey, a tranquil scene.
Each face glows with warmth and grace,
In early echoes, we find our place.

Laughter mingles with the soft breeze,
As harmony dances among the trees.
Hands reaching out, together strong,
We build a world where we belong.

Colors burst in a vibrant mix,
Nature's palette, a joyful fix.
In every glance, a moment to share,
In these echoes, love fills the air.

As the sun climbs, shadows recede,
Embracing each, planting the seed.
In early echoes, hearts align,
A tapestry woven, so divine.

Waking Dreams

In the stillness of the night,
Stars twinkle with a soft light.
Whispers of hope fill the air,
Promising dreams beyond compare.

As dawn breaks, colors unfold,
Stories of courage yet untold.
Each moment, a canvas divine,
In waking dreams, our spirits shine.

Clouds drift slowly, dreams take flight,
Chasing shadows, embracing light.
With open hearts, we seek and find,
The threads of destiny intertwined.

Life's symphony plays on repeat,
In every heartbeat, a rhythmic beat.
We chase the dawn, refusing to sleep,
In waking dreams, our souls leap.

As day wanes, reflections stir,
In the quiet, we begin to blur.
Transcending the bounds of night and day,
In waking dreams, we find our way.

Threads of Light

Threads of light weave through the trees,
Dancing petals kiss the breeze.
Nature's artistry, a wondrous sight,
In every flicker, whispers ignite.

Shadows lengthen as day drifts low,
Moments captured in a golden glow.
Each thread connects our heart's delight,
Binding us in this gentle light.

Voices echo in harmony sweet,
A symphony that cannot be beat.
We are the fabric, rich and bright,
Intertwined in the threads of light.

As twilight beckons, stars appear,
Guiding our path, dispelling fear.
Together we shine, bold and bright,
With every heartbeat, threads unite.

In the tapestry of life we find,
Connections deep, forever entwined.
In every moment, spirit in flight,
Celebrating the threads of light.

The Canvas of Dawn

Each brushstroke paints the sky,
A palette of crimson and gold.
The day awakens with a sigh,
Embracing stories untold.

The shadows dance with the light,
As night slowly curls away.
A canvas filled with delight,
Promises of a brand new day.

Birds take flight in jubilant song,
Announcing the dawn's embrace.
Nature joins, where all belong,
In this luminous space.

Golden hues stretch far and wide,
Revealing the world anew.
Hope and dreams side by side,
In the morning's gentle view.

Each moment a fleeting chance,
To seize the day and engage.
In this vibrant, bright romance,
Life begins on a fresh page.

Connections in the Glow

In the twilight's gentle embrace,
Hearts intertwine and align.
Every smile shares a trace,
Of love in the soft decline.

Flickers of light draw us near,
A warmth that we can't ignore.
In the silence, we can hear,
The whispers of something more.

Laughter dances in the air,
As shadows softly fall.
Moments cherished, beyond compare,
Creating bonds that enthrall.

Through the glow of fleeting time,
Connections deepen and grow.
In rhythm, our spirits climb,
Finding peace in the flow.

Every glance, a story shared,
Written in the light of the night.
In the warmth, we're wholly bared,
Together, we shine so bright.

In the Light of New Beginnings

With dawn's first light, we rise,
Casting off the weight of night.
A world anew before our eyes,
Hope ignites with pure delight.

Each step taken feels so bold,
A journey we embark upon.
The tales of courage yet untold,
In the warmth of the sun's dawn.

Fresh beginnings greet the soul,
With every heartbeat's soft embrace.
Together, we can feel whole,
In life's ever-changing race.

The horizon paints with bright hues,
A promise of what's yet to come.
With every moment, we choose,
To step forward, overcome.

In this light, we find our way,
Guided by dreams we ignite.
Each new dawn, a canvas lay,
For visions taking flight.

Whispers of the Awakening

A gentle breeze stirs the leaves,
As dawn unfolds its tender grace.
Nature stirs, and softly breathes,
In the light of this sacred place.

With every chirp and rustling sound,
The world begins to awaken.
Life's wonders, both lost and found,
In the stillness unshaken.

Colors bloom with brilliant flair,
Painting the canvas of the day.
The fragrance of blossoms in the air,
Whispers of hope on display.

Eyes meet as the sun ascends,
Promises linger in the glow.
Hearts unite as love transcends,
In the warmth of the warm tableau.

Embrace the moments soft and rare,
As life whispers, beckoning near.
In the awakening, we declare,
Together, love conquers fear.

Embraces at Daybreak

The dawn breaks softly with gentle light,
A whisper of warmth in the cool morning air.
Arms of the sun embrace the night,
As dreams fade gently, no longer there.

Colors dance softly across the sky,
As shadows retreat from the light so bright.
Birds awaken, their chorus a sigh,
In the tender embrace of day's first light.

Morning dew glistens on blades of green,
Every petal unfurls with a quiet grace.
In this sacred hour, the world feels serene,
Each heartbeat echoes in nature's embrace.

A canvas of hope, painted anew,
Every moment a gift, a chance to start.
In these embraces, the soul will renew,
With the sun's gentle warmth, we mend our heart.

So let us cherish each dawn as it wakes,
With a promise of joy and moments to share.
In the magic of morning, our spirit awakes,
Embraces at daybreak, beyond compare.

Echoes of Light

In the still of the dawn, a whispering glow,
Light spills softly on the waking earth.
Each flicker and shimmer, a story to show,
Of dreams that awaken with the day's birth.

Through branches and leaves, the sun peeks in,
Casting shadows that dance in delight.
The world is alive, shedding darkness and sin,
As nature rejoices in the echoes of light.

With each gentle ray, new beginnings rise,
A tapestry woven with threads of the sun.
In silence, we listen to truth in disguise,
For life is a journey, and we are but one.

The laughter of children, the songs of the breeze,
Are echoes that linger, sweet notes in the air.
In moments like these, troubles find ease,
In harmony's melody, our burdens we share.

So dance with the shadows that flicker and gleam,
Embrace every moment, let joy take its flight.
In the heart of the day, sweet freedom will beam,
Reminding us softly, we're part of the light.

Soft Murmurs of Morning

In the hush of the morn, a whispering breeze,
Gentle rustles in the leaves overhead.
The world awakes softly, as if to tease,
With sweet murmurs of life where silence once tread.

The coffee pot simmers, a fragrant delight,
As sunlight spills gold through the window's embrace.
Each moment a treasure, so warm and so bright,
In the soft murmurs of morning, we find our place.

Birds chirp their secrets, a symphony clear,
Painting the canvas of blue skies above.
With every soft note, we hold what is dear,
In the embrace of the morning, wrapped in love.

The dew-kissed grass glistens like diamonds, aglow,
As flowers stretch out, yawning, waking to light.
A gentle reminder of all things that grow,
In the soft murmurs of morning, life takes flight.

So let us be present, in quiet allure,
With hearts open wide to embrace what's in sight.
For in these sweet moments, our souls feel secure,
In soft murmurs of morning, the world feels right.

Horizon's Heartbeat

The horizon stretches, painted in hues,
Where sky meets the earth in a lover's embrace.
With each passing moment, the light renews,
In the dance of the day, a tender grace.

Mountains stand proud, against skies unfurling,
As rivers weave stories, forever they flow.
In nature's symphony, hearts are unfurling,
With each breath we take, the world's rhythm we know.

The sun rises higher, igniting the day,
Casting shadows that flicker with life on the land.
In the warmth of its glow, find your way,
For horizon's heartbeat is ever so grand.

Clouds drift like whispers, ephemeral dreams,
Painting soft shadows that dance and entwine.
In this vivid tapestry, nothing's as it seems,
Yet in each fleeting moment, your spirit can shine.

So cherish the journey, this heartbeat divine,
With the horizon as witness, our souls take flight.
For in every sunrise, a new hope we find,
In the embrace of the dawn, we are wrapped in light.

Awakening Whispers

Softly the dawn begins to break,
Gentle whispers in the trees.
Nature stirs with every shake,
A symphony carried on the breeze.

Sunlight weaves through curtains drawn,
Dreams dissolve in morning's glow.
New beginnings greet the dawn,
As shadows fade, and colors flow.

Birds above begin to sing,
Melodies of hope and cheer.
In their song, a new heart's spring,
Promises of joy ever near.

Fields awaken, dew on blades,
Each drop reflects the sun's warm rays.
A dance of life in gentle shades,
As night retreats, and daylight plays.

With each breath, the world ignites,
Vibrant hues of gold and green.
Embrace the beauty of these sights,
In this moment, we are seen.

The Dawn's Embrace

Around the world, the light cascades,
A tender touch, a sweet caress.
Golden fingers warm the glades,
In the dawn, we find our rest.

Silhouettes of trees arise,
Against the canvas painted bright.
Awake beneath the endless skies,
Embraced by morning's soft delight.

Whispers of the day unfold,
Each ray a promise, pure and true.
With stories waiting to be told,
In the light, our dreams renew.

Moments linger in the air,
Captured briefly, shy and bold.
A heartbeat in the stillness there,
As dawn's embrace begins to hold.

In this space, our souls align,
Connected by the golden thread.
We cherish every sign divine,
In dawn's embrace, we're freely led.

Threads of First Light

A tapestry of colors spread,
Threads of light weave through the sky.
Morning whispers, gently said,
Kissing dreams as they pass by.

On winds of change, the echoes play,
Where shadows meet the edge of day.
A canvas bright in hues of gray,
Threads of first light lead the way.

With every breath, the world unfolds,
Rich with hope, in warmth enclosed.
Stories in the light, retold,
In each heartbeat, life imposed.

Gentle dew on petals gleams,
Promises of what's to come.
Awakening to vibrant dreams,
Spreading hope before the sun.

Threads of first light, pure and bright,
Guide our spirits, drawing near.
In the stillness of the night,
We find our strength, we face our fear.

Morning's Gentle Call

The world awakens, soft and slow,
In the beauty of the morn.
Each petal glistens, set aglow,
From the quiet, life is born.

A chime of leaves in gentle air,
Birdsongs weave a joyful sound.
Nature's breath is rich and rare,
In this moment, peace is found.

Clouds drift softly, dreams within,
Every moment, pure delight.
As light spills forth and shadows thin,
We embrace the morning's light.

With open arms, we greet the day,
Casting worries far and wide.
In morning's warmth, we choose to stay,
With love and hope as our guide.

Each heartbeat echoes in the still,
Together, we rise, we stand tall.
Awakened now, we find our will,
In morning's gentle, familiar call.

Dawn's Embrace

Softly breaks the dawn's first light,
A gentle kiss, all dark takes flight.
Birds begin their morning song,
In this world where dreams belong.

The sky blushes with hues so bright,
Golden whispers chase the night.
Every shadow starts to fade,
In the warmth, new hopes are made.

Leaves rustle in the waking breeze,
Nature stirs with graceful ease.
Flowers bloom in radiant cheer,
As the sun draws ever near.

Moments pause, in tranquil grace,
Heartbeats echo, time's embrace.
In the stillness, magic flows,
In every pause, the spirit grows.

A canvas vast, of dreams unfurled,
In dawn's embrace, a brand-new world.
With each ray, life's spark ignites,
Together, dance in morning lights.

Threads of Light

In the fabric of the morn,
Golden threads of light are born.
Stitching dreams with radiant care,
Weaving hope into the air.

A tapestry of vibrant hues,
Painting skies with joyful views.
Each beam dances, soft and bright,
Guiding souls towards the light.

Whispers carried on the breeze,
Secrets shared among the trees.
Nature's voice begins to sing,
Awakening the love of spring.

With each stitch, a promise made,
In the light, all fears are laid.
Threads of hope, they intertwine,
Binding hearts in love divine.

So let us walk, hand in hand,
Through the beauty, across the land.
With every step, our spirits rise,
In threads of light, we find our skies.

Awakening Whispers

Quiet murmurs greet the day,
Softly drifting, come what may.
Nature calls with gentle hands,
Awakening in silent lands.

A breeze passes, whispers clear,
Carrying secrets, drawing near.
In the stillness, heartbeats blend,
Each moment breathes, a time to mend.

Shadows lift, as light takes form,
In the warmth, we find our norm.
Rustling leaves, a symphony,
Awakening the world, so free.

With every step, the earth responds,
Filling souls with hopeful bonds.
In this union, spirits dance,
Awakening in life's romance.

So listen close to whispers low,
In their rhythm, let love flow.
Together we shall find our way,
Awakening with each new day.

The First Glow

The first glow breaks the silent night,
Filling hearts with pure delight.
A promise wrapped in amber light,
Glistening hills, a beautiful sight.

With every moment, shadows flee,
Painting dreams where we feel free.
Crickets hush, the world grows still,
As morning whispers promise thrill.

The horizon blushes, tender and bright,
A canvas fresh, of day and light.
Waking souls to life anew,
In golden beams, a world in view.

Rays touch softly, gently flow,
In every heart, a spark we sow.
Together, bask in dawn's embrace,
In the first glow, we find our place.

So let us rise with spirits free,
Chasing dreams like waves at sea.
For in this moment, all can see,
The first glow holds our destiny.

Whispered Promises at Daybreak

In the hush before the dawn,
Soft whispers in the air,
Fleeting dreams gently drawn,
Hope rising from despair.

Golden rays begin to spill,
Painting shadows on the ground,
Each heartbeat, calm and still,
In this peace, love is found.

Morning dew on petals lie,
Nature wakes with tender grace,
A sweet serenade, the sky,
Beckons all to find their place.

Birds take flight on silver wings,
Chasing echoes of the night,
Every note that nature sings,
Brings forth warmth, dispels the fright.

As the sun climbs up so high,
Promises made in hushed tones,
In the brilliance of the sky,
Together, never alone.

Fusions of Light

Shimmers dance in twilight's glow,
Merging colors, warm embrace,
In the darkness, seeds we sow,
From the shadows, dreams we trace.

Fires sparked by whispered dreams,
Cascading hues in night's delight,
Every flicker softly gleams,
Bringing hope, piercing the night.

Stars collide in cosmic play,
Creating paths for hearts to roam,
In a world where night meets day,
Every pulse feels like a home.

The canvas of the fading light,
Brushed with love and heart's desire,
In the stillness, names take flight,
Echoing through realms of fire.

With each spark, new worlds unfurl,
In the night's gentle embrace,
Together we shall spin and twirl,
Fusions of light, time and space.

Dawn's Unspoken Language

Misty breaths of morning air,
Cloaked in gold, the silence sings,
Nature speaks without a care,
Through the rise of wondrous things.

Every leaf a story weaves,
Glimmers caught in sunlight's gaze,
In the stillness, heart believes,
In the magic of these days.

Mountains stand with watchful eyes,
Guardians of the waking light,
As the sun begins to rise,
Shadows fade, embracing bright.

Unseen whispers in the breeze,
Carry tales from yesteryear,
In the rustle of the trees,
Dawn's soft voice, vibrant and clear.

With each heartbeat, life anew,
Promises in the morning's kiss,
In this dance of me and you,
Dawn's unspoken, sweet, abyss.

Threads of Vibrance

Woven tales of radiant hue,
Interlaced with dreams that soar,
In every thread, a piece of you,
In the fabric, we explore.

Colors burst in joyful sway,
Tangled vines and blossoms sweet,
In the brightness of the day,
Life's tapestry, rich and complete.

With hands skilled and hearts aligned,
We craft each moment, bold and bright,
In the patterns of love defined,
Every stitch shines with delight.

Embers glow, they softly bind,
The past, the present, dreams that gleam,
In this masterpiece we find,
A world alive, a shared dream.

Through the loom of time we weave,
Every fiber speaks of grace,
In this dance, we shall believe,
Threads of vibrance, time and space.

New Horizons Unfold

In the dawn's embrace, we rise,
Chasing dreams beyond the skies.
With every step, the world expands,
A tapestry woven, in hopeful hands.

Mountains call with silent grace,
In rivers deep, our hearts find place.
New paths await, the brave will roam,
Together we build, a journey home.

Whispers of the winds ignite,
In the stillness, we find our light.
Embracing change, we break the mold,
New horizons, brave and bold.

Through valleys wide and forests old,
Our stories merge, forever told.
With starry nights, we weave our fate,
In unity, we celebrate.

So here we stand, hand in hand,
With open hearts, we're free and grand.
The future sparkles, bright and clear,
New horizons draw us near.

The Language of Light

Soft beams dance upon the ground,
In silence, beauty can be found.
Whispers of the day ignite,
In the gentle language of light.

Colors bloom in morning's grace,
Each hue reflects a warm embrace.
With every ray, a story glows,
In radiant paths, our spirit flows.

Shadows play with dreams anew,
In twilight's hue, we find the true.
Glimmers of hope in the fading day,
In the language of light, we sway.

Yet when the night begins to fall,
Stars ignite, we heed their call.
In cosmic realms, our hearts take flight,
Connected through the endless night.

So let us dance in brilliance' glow,
Embracing all that we can know.
In each glimmer, a spark of delight,
Forever bound in the language of light.

Silhouettes in Amber

As the sun dips low, shadows grow,
Silhouettes dance in amber's glow.
Fleeting moments, soft and sweet,
A memory made, a heart's retreat.

Leaves are painted in gold and rose,
Each whisper of the evening flows.
In twilight's arms, we find our way,
A gentle sigh, the end of day.

Underneath the twilight's watch,
Time stands still, it dares not botch.
In stillness felt, the world seems bright,
As dreams entwine with fading light.

The stars emerge, like wishes spun,
And beckon us to play, to run.
United in the dusk's embrace,
In amber shades, we find our place.

So let us linger, hand in hand,
In silken twilight, we understand.
With every heartbeat, every sigh,
Silhouettes in amber, we soar high.

Awakening Together

In the stillness before the dawn,
Nature whispers, life reborn.
With every breath, we feel the change,
Awakening spirits, vast and strange.

Eyes open wide to a brand new day,
Together we rise, come what may.
In shared laughter, our hearts unite,
Awakening together, pure delight.

Each moment blooms, a vibrant hue,
In unity, all things are true.
Hand in hand, we'll forge our way,
In harmony, we choose to stay.

Mountains high and valleys low,
With courage found, we'll always grow.
In the dance of life, we take our part,
Awakening together, heart to heart.

So let us journey, side by side,
With hope and love as our guide.
In the embrace of a world so wide,
Awakening together, we shall abide.

Daybreak Conversations

In whispers soft, the dawn will break,
As shadows fade, new chances wake.
With golden hues, the skies unfold,
Each moment's promise, brave and bold.

We share our dreams with morning's light,
As day begins, we take our flight.
With laughter ringing, hearts set free,
Together we write our history.

The world a canvas, fresh and bright,
Brushstrokes of hope in a blushing sight.
We speak of wonders yet to come,
Our spirits dance to freedom's drum.

Each thought a treasure, pure and true,
In every silence, I find you.
We weave our tales, both old and new,
In daybreak's glow, our bond we grew.

So let us cherish every word,
For in our voices, dreams are stirred.
With daybreak's chat, the world awakes,
In unity, our path we make.

Hues of Hope

In twilight's breath, the colors rise,
A canvas painted in soft sighs.
With strokes of gold, the day is born,
In every shade, a dream is worn.

The sky a tapestry of light,
Each hue a promise, bold and bright.
We linger where the shadows part,
Finding solace in every heart.

Through whispers soft, the colors blend,
With nature's brush, our spirits mend.
In vibrant tones, we find our trust,
In the bursts of life, hope turns to dust.

With azure depths and fiery red,
The palette speaks where silence led.
Each moment painted in our minds,
In hues of hope, our love unwinds.

So let us cherish every shade,
In life's great art, our paths are laid.
With brushes held, we dare to dream,
In every heart, a vibrant gleam.

Embracing the New Dawn

With morning's light, we rise anew,
Embracing hope in each soft hue.
The world awakens, fresh and bright,
As shadows flee from dawn's first light.

In gentle rays, our fears dissolve,
We find the strength as we evolve.
With open arms, we greet the day,
In every challenge, we find our way.

As whispers swell in morning's song,
Together here, where we belong.
The past behind, the future clear,
In unity, we conquer fear.

With laughter shared and tears of joy,
Each moment cherished, life's sweet ploy.
We write our story, bold and true,
In every heartbeat, me and you.

So let the dawn's embrace be ours,
In every detail, in every hour.
Together we'll stand, hand in hand,
Embracing the dawn, our dreams expand.

Where Light Meets Land

Upon the shore, where waters gleam,
The sun will rise, the world a dream.
In vibrant hues, the dawn will show,
Where light and land in beauty flow.

The waves in rhythm, soft and sweet,
A dance of nature, pure and neat.
With every tide, our worries cease,
In harmony, we find our peace.

In quiet moments, hearts align,
Where sea meets sky, your hand in mine.
The vast horizon calls us near,
In every whisper, you are here.

As light embraces land's soft curves,
Our souls immerse in gentle swerves.
In every glance, a promise made,
In sunset's glow, our fears do fade.

So let us wander, lost in time,
Where light meets land, a perfect rhyme.
With every step, our spirits soar,
In this embrace, we yearn for more.

Chasing the First Rays

Beneath the veil of dawn's embrace,
Golden beams begin to race.
Whispers of light, soft and slow,
Awakening life from shadows below.

Birds sing sweetly, take their flight,
Nature stirs in morning light.
Each petal glistens with dew's kiss,
In this moment, there's pure bliss.

The sky blushes with hues of gold,
A painter's dream, vibrant and bold.
As sun climbs high, shadows retreat,
Joy in the air, life feels complete.

Chasing rays, we find our way,
In the warmth of a brand new day.
Hearts open wide, ready to soar,
With the first light, we yearn for more.

Morning's Sacred Symphony

Morning breaks with a gentle sigh,
Nature wakes beneath the sky.
Each note plays a tranquil tune,
Harmony hums to the sun and moon.

Rustling leaves join the refrain,
A breeze dances, soft and plain.
Birdsong rises, pure and clear,
Every melody draws us near.

The world stirs to this sacred sound,
Beauty in stillness, all around.
Colors blend in a vibrant array,
An orchestra for the break of day.

With each breath, we play our part,
A symphony that warms the heart.
In morning's light, we find our grace,
Each moment, a sweet embrace.

Echoes of Daylight

In the hush before the dawn,
Echoes linger, softly drawn.
Whispers of the night fade away,
As daylight dances, bold and gay.

Crickets cease their evening song,
A new day beckons, bright and strong.
Lights of dawn touch every face,
Guiding hearts to a warm embrace.

Footsteps mark the fresh, cool ground,
Hope awakens in each sound.
With every breath, we rise anew,
Chasing echoes, vibrant and true.

The sun spills gold across the land,
A sacred gift from nature's hand.
In the light, we find our way,
Echoes of a brighter day.

The Day's First Breath

A silent hush, the world awaits,
The sun ascends, the darkness abates.
Softly unfurls a golden ray,
Life awakens at the start of the day.

Morning mist dances in the air,
Nature stirs with utmost care.
Each flower opens, a gentle sigh,
Breath of dawn as time drifts by.

Cool winds whisper, secrets shared,
In this moment, hearts are bared.
The sky blushes in hues of rose,
As tranquil beauty deftly flows.

The day begins, a canvas bright,
With strokes of joy, pure delight.
Embrace the magic, take a chance,
In the day's first breath, we dance.

Unfolding Cherished Moments

In a quiet room we sit,
Laughter shared, a gentle wit.
Time weaves memories with grace,
Each glance reveals a treasured space.

Soft whispers under starlit skies,
With every secret, the heart replies.
Cups of tea and warm embraces,
In these moments, love's traces.

Through seasons passed, we weave our tales,
In every word, affection hails.
Captured smiles and tender sighs,
In cherished moments, life never lies.

The clock ticks slow, yet time takes flight,
Holding close this tranquil night.
As the dawn begins to bloom,
We carry love, dispelling gloom.

In memories carved, we find our song,
A melody where we belong.
With every heart that softly beats,
Cherished moments, life completes.

Celestial Conversations

Underneath the sprawling night,
Stars converse in twinkling light.
Galaxies swirl in a gentle hum,
Whispers of worlds where dreams come from.

Moonbeams dance on silken waves,
Each glimmer tells what the cosmos saves.
Planets spin in harmonious grace,
In celestial talks, we find our place.

Comets trail with tales untold,
Secrets of time, both new and old.
Infinity calls with a voice so sweet,
In stardust paths, our spirits meet.

Constellations sketch our fate,
In patterns vast, both small and great.
Galactic dreams weave through the night,
In every glance, a spark ignites.

Beneath this vast and endless dome,
We seek the void, and make it home.
In celestial conversations we soar,
To the universe, forevermore.

The Beauty of Beginnings

A sunrise breaks the silent kiss,
Each ray unfolds, a golden bliss.
In tender hues, the world awakes,
A fresh canvas, as daylight breaks.

Golden buds on branches sway,
Whispers of spring, a new ballet.
Hope emerges from the frost,
In beginnings, we find what was lost.

Songs of laughter fill the air,
New friendships bloom, a joyous flair.
Hearts ignite with fervent dreams,
In the beauty of beginnings, hope gleams.

Each step taken, a story spun,
A path unfolding, life's great run.
In every heartbeat, past and now,
The beauty of beginnings takes a bow.

In the tender light of each new start,
We weave our tales, we play our part.
With open arms, we greet the dawn,
In every breath, a beautiful yawn.

Illuminated Paths

Beneath the canopy of stars,
We wander paths, secluded scars.
With lanterns bright, we chase the night,
In illuminated dreams, take flight.

Each corner turned reveals the glow,
Of hidden trails that gently flow.
In whispered winds, the secrets tell,
Of journeys paved, where spirits dwell.

Footsteps echo on this way,
Guided softly by the play.
On illuminated paths we dare,
To search for wonders lingering there.

The moon's soft light, a beacon's blaze,
Navigating life's twisting maze.
In shadows cast, we find our heart,
As illuminated dreams impart.

Together we tread, hand in hand,
Finding solace in the land.
On paths aglow, we face the night,
With love to guide us, pure and bright.

www.ingramcontent.com/pod-product-compliance
Ingram Content Group UK Ltd.
Pitfield, Milton Keynes, MK11 3LW, UK
UKHW021942200125
4187UKWH00037B/759